The Colasante Sales Method: Mastering the Art of Selling

By Anthony Colasante

I0401351

Table of Contents

1. Prospecting Like a Pro
   - **Identifying Your Target Market**
   - **Effective Lead Generation Strategies**
   - **Using Social Media and Technology**
1. **The Art of the Cold Call**
   - **Preparing for Cold Calls**
   - **Crafting Your Pitch**
   - **Handling Objections and Staying Persistent**
1. **Mastering the Follow-Up**
   - **Importance of Follow-Up**
   - **Creating a Follow-Up System**
   - **Techniques for Effective Follow-Up**
1. **Presenting with Confidence**
   - **Crafting Compelling Presentations**
   - **Engaging Your Audience**
   - **Using Stories and Visuals**
1. **Closing the Deal**
   - **Recognizing Buying Signals**
   -

Introduction

Welcome to the Colasante Method

Welcome to a transformative journey in sales mastery using the Colasante Method. This method is designed to elevate your sales skills, increase your effectiveness, and ultimately, boost your revenue. By adopting the principles and techniques laid out in this ebook, you will gain insights into the art and science of selling, grounded in the rich experiences and proven strategies developed by Colasante.

Overview of the Colasante Sales Philosophy

The Colasante Sales Philosophy centers around understanding and addressing the unique needs of each customer. It is built on the foundation of value-based selling, where the focus is on creating and communicating value rather than merely pushing products. This approach not only builds trust and rapport with clients but also positions you as a trusted advisor rather than just a salesperson. The philosophy emphasizes persistence, a positive mindset, and the continuous refinement of your sales techniques to adapt to the ever-evolving market dynamics.

Importance of Mastering Sales

Mastering sales is more than just achieving targets; it's about developing a skill set that will serve you in every aspect of your professional and personal life. Sales skills are essential in navigating business landscapes, negotiating deals, and fostering relationships. By mastering sales, you become adept at identifying opportunities, understanding customer pain points, and providing solutions that resonate with their needs. This not only leads to increased sales but also to long-term customer loyalty and business growth.

Who is Anthony Colasante?

Anthony Colasante, a seasoned sales professional with a diverse background in various sales domains, has distilled his extensive experience into this comprehensive guide. With a career that spans retail, door-to-door sales, business-to-business interactions, and high-stakes environments such as real estate and funeral services, Colasante has honed a unique approach to sales. His journey from a college student uncertain about his future to a top-performing sales leader is a testament to the effectiveness of the methods you will learn in this ebook. Through this guide, Colasante aims to share the lessons, strategies, and techniques that have driven his success, empowering you to achieve your own sales goals.

Chapter 2 - Understanding the Sales Process

The Sales Cycle

Understanding the sales process is crucial for any sales professional. The sales cycle is the series of predictable phases required to sell a product or service. The cycle is broken down into several stages:

1. **Prospecting**: Identifying potential customers.
2. **Initial Contact**: Making the first connection with potential customers.
3. **Qualification**: Determining if the prospect has a need for your product and the means to buy it.
4. **Presentation**: Demonstrating the value of your product or service to the prospect.
5. **Handling Objections**: Addressing any concerns or questions the prospect may have.
6. **Closing**: Finalizing the sale.
7. **Follow-Up**: Ensuring customer satisfaction and identifying opportunities for additional sales.

Each stage requires specific strategies and techniques to move the prospect closer to a purchase decision.

Key Components of Successful Sales

Successful sales hinge on several key components:

1. **Preparation**: Understanding your product, market, and customer needs.
2. **Active Listening**: Paying close attention to the prospect's needs and concerns.
3. **Value Proposition**: Clearly articulating how your product or service solves the prospect's problem.
4. **Building Rapport**: Establishing a connection and trust with the prospect.

5. **Persistence**: Consistently following up and staying engaged with the prospect.
6. **Adaptability**: Being flexible and responsive to the prospect's needs and feedback.

By focusing on these components, you can improve your effectiveness at each stage of the sales cycle.

Setting Clear Goals and Objectives

Setting clear goals and objectives is essential for guiding your sales efforts and measuring your progress. Here are some steps to help you set effective goals:

1. **Define Specific Objectives**: Outline what you want to achieve, whether it's a certain number of sales, revenue targets, or market penetration.
2. **Make Goals Measurable**: Use quantifiable metrics to track your progress. For example, aiming to increase sales by 20% within six months.
3. **Ensure Goals are Achievable**: Set realistic targets that challenge you but are within reach.
4. **Relevant Goals**: Align your objectives with broader business goals and market realities.
5. **Time-Bound Targets**: Set deadlines for achieving your goals to maintain a sense of urgency and focus.

By setting SMART (Specific, Measurable, Achievable, Relevant, Time-bound) goals, you can create a clear roadmap for your sales efforts and stay motivated and accountable.

The Power of a Positive Mindset

A positive mindset is a powerful tool in sales. It can help you stay motivated, overcome challenges, and build better relationships with your customers. Here are some ways to cultivate a positive mindset:

1. **Self-Belief**: Confidence in your abilities can drive your performance. Visualize your success and believe in your skills.
2. **Resilience**: Sales often involve rejection. Develop resilience to bounce back from setbacks and keep pushing forward.
3. **Positive Attitude**: Approach every interaction with optimism. A positive attitude can be contagious and help build rapport with prospects.
4. **Continuous Learning**: View every experience, whether successful or not, as a learning opportunity. This growth mindset will help you improve over time.
5. **Gratitude**: Appreciate the opportunities you have and the progress you make. Gratitude can boost your overall happiness and productivity.

Maintaining a positive mindset will not only improve your sales performance but also enhance your overall well-being.

Developing Resilience and Persistence

Resilience and persistence are crucial traits for successful salespeople. Here are some strategies to develop these qualities:

1. **Embrace Challenges**: View obstacles as opportunities to learn and grow. Challenges can help you develop new skills and strategies.
2. **Setbacks as Learning Experiences**: Analyze setbacks to understand what went wrong and how to improve. Use these insights to refine your approach.
3. **Stay Focused on Goals**: Keep your long-term objectives in mind to stay motivated during tough times.
4. **Seek Support**: Build a network of colleagues, mentors, and friends who can offer advice, encouragement, and support.

5. **Practice Patience**: Understand that success takes time and persistence. Stay patient and keep working towards your goals.

By developing resilience and persistence, you can navigate the ups and downs of sales more effectively and achieve sustained success.

Overcoming Rejection and Failure

Rejection and failure are inevitable in sales. How you handle them can make a significant difference in your success. Here are some tips to help you overcome rejection and failure:

1. **Don't Take It Personally**: Understand that rejection is not a reflection of your worth. It's often due to factors beyond your control.
2. **Learn from Each Experience**: Analyze rejections to identify patterns and areas for improvement. Use this feedback to refine your approach.
3. **Stay Positive**: Maintain a positive attitude and focus on the next opportunity rather than dwelling on past failures.
4. **Build a Support System**: Surround yourself with supportive colleagues and mentors who can offer guidance and encouragement.
5. **Keep Moving Forward**: Don't let rejection derail your efforts. Keep prospecting, following up, and refining your approach.

By developing strategies to handle rejection and failure, you can maintain your momentum and continue moving towards your sales goals.

By understanding the sales process and mastering its key components, you can enhance your effectiveness and achieve greater success in your sales career. The Colasante Method provides a structured approach to help you navigate each stage of the sales cycle, build strong relationships with customers, and close more deals.

Chapter 2: Understanding the Sales Process

The Sales Cycle

Understanding the sales cycle is crucial for any sales professional. It encompasses the various stages that a prospect goes through before becoming a customer. The sales cycle is not a one-size-fits-all process; it can vary depending on the industry, product, or service. However, the fundamental stages remain consistent. These stages are:

1. **Prospecting**: This is the initial stage where you identify potential customers. Effective prospecting involves researching and identifying your target market. Use various tools and techniques such as social media, networking events, and referrals to find potential leads.
2. **Initial Contact**: Once you have identified potential prospects, the next step is to make the initial contact. This can be through a phone call, email, or face-to-face meeting. The goal is to introduce yourself and your company, and to gauge the prospect's interest in your product or service.
3. **Qualification**: Not every prospect will be a good fit for your product or service. During the qualification stage, you need to determine whether the prospect has a need for your product, the budget to purchase it, and the authority to make the buying decision. Ask probing questions to understand their pain points and requirements.
4. **Presentation**: If the prospect is qualified, the next step is to present your product or service. Tailor your presentation to address the specific needs and pain points of the prospect. Use stories, case studies, and demonstrations to show how your product can solve their problems.

5. **Handling Objections**: Prospects will often have objections or concerns about your product or service. It's essential to handle these objections professionally and confidently. Listen to their concerns, acknowledge them, and provide solutions or evidence to alleviate their doubts.
6. **Closing**: This is the most critical stage of the sales cycle. Closing the deal involves getting the prospect to make a commitment to purchase. Use various closing techniques such as the assumptive close, the urgency close, or the option close to seal the deal.
7. **Follow-Up**: After the sale is made, it's important to follow up with the customer to ensure they are satisfied with their purchase. This helps build a long-term relationship and can lead to repeat business and referrals.

Key Components of Successful Sales

To be successful in sales, you need to master several key components:

1. **Communication Skills**: Effective communication is at the heart of sales. You need to be able to convey your message clearly and persuasively. This includes both verbal and non-verbal communication. Pay attention to your body language, tone of voice, and active listening skills.
2. **Product Knowledge**: You must have an in-depth understanding of the product or service you are selling. This includes its features, benefits, and how it compares to competitors. The more knowledgeable you are, the more confident you will be in presenting your product and handling objections.
3. **Customer Focus**: Successful salespeople are customer-focused. They understand the needs and

pain points of their prospects and tailor their approach accordingly. Building rapport and trust with your prospects is crucial for long-term success.

4. **Time Management**: Sales is a fast-paced profession, and effective time management is essential. Prioritize your tasks, set goals, and use tools such as CRM systems to manage your pipeline and follow-up activities efficiently.

5. **Resilience and Persistence**: Sales can be challenging, and you will face rejection and setbacks. Successful salespeople are resilient and persistent. They learn from their failures and keep pushing forward.

Setting Clear Goals and Objectives

Setting clear goals and objectives is vital for success in sales. Goals provide direction and motivation, and they help you measure your progress. Here are some tips for setting effective sales goals:

1. **Specific**: Your goals should be specific and clearly defined. Instead of setting a vague goal like "increase sales," set a specific goal such as "increase sales by 20% in the next quarter."

2. **Measurable**: Your goals should be measurable so that you can track your progress. Use metrics such as revenue, number of new customers, or conversion rates to measure your success.

3. **Achievable**: Set realistic and achievable goals. While it's important to challenge yourself, setting goals that are too ambitious can lead to frustration and burnout.

4. **Relevant**: Your goals should be relevant to your overall sales strategy and objectives. Ensure that they align with your company's mission and vision.

5. **Time-Bound**: Set a deadline for achieving your goals. This creates a sense of urgency and helps you stay focused and motivated.

Building a Winning Attitude

A winning attitude is essential for success in sales. It involves maintaining a positive mindset, staying motivated, and being persistent. Here are some tips for building a winning attitude:

1. **Positive Mindset**: Cultivate a positive mindset by focusing on your strengths and successes. Surround yourself with positive influences and avoid negative self-talk.
2. **Motivation**: Find what motivates you and use it to fuel your drive. This could be financial rewards, personal growth, or the satisfaction of helping customers.
3. **Persistence**: Sales requires persistence. Don't give up after a few rejections. Learn from your experiences and keep pushing forward.
4. **Continuous Learning**: Invest in your personal and professional development. Attend training sessions, read books, and seek feedback to continuously improve your skills.
5. **Work-Life Balance**: Maintaining a healthy work-life balance is crucial for long-term success. Take time to relax, recharge, and spend time with loved ones. This will help you stay motivated and prevent burnout.

By mastering these fundamentals, you will be well on your way to becoming a successful salesperson. The next chapters will delve deeper into specific sales techniques and strategies to further enhance your skills and effectiveness.

Chapter 3: Building a Winning Attitude

A winning attitude is a cornerstone of success in sales. It is what separates top performers from the rest and drives consistent achievements even in the face of challenges. Building and maintaining a winning attitude requires a combination of positive mindset, motivation, resilience, and continuous improvement. In this chapter, we will explore the components of a winning attitude and provide practical tips to help you cultivate and sustain it.

The Power of a Positive Mindset

A positive mindset is essential for overcoming obstacles and staying motivated. Here are key aspects to develop and maintain a positive mindset:

1. **Focus on Solutions, Not Problems**: When faced with challenges, shift your focus from the problem to finding solutions. This proactive approach keeps you motivated and engaged in overcoming obstacles.
2. **Practice Gratitude**: Regularly acknowledging what you are grateful for helps maintain a positive outlook. Start each day by reflecting on positive aspects of your life and career.
3. **Visualize Success**: Visualization is a powerful tool. Take time each day to imagine achieving your goals and the positive outcomes that will result. This practice reinforces a positive attitude and strengthens your determination.
4. **Surround Yourself with Positivity**: The people you associate with have a significant impact on your mindset. Surround yourself with positive, supportive individuals who inspire and uplift you.
5. **Positive Self-Talk**: Replace negative thoughts with positive affirmations. Remind yourself of your

strengths and past successes. This will boost your confidence and reinforce a winning attitude.

Developing Resilience and Persistence

Resilience and persistence are critical components of a winning attitude. They enable you to bounce back from setbacks and keep pushing forward. Here's how to develop these traits:

1. **Embrace Failure as a Learning Opportunity**: Every failure is a chance to learn and grow. Analyze what went wrong, extract lessons, and apply them to future endeavors. This approach turns setbacks into stepping stones for success.
2. **Set Realistic Expectations**: Understand that not every prospect will turn into a sale and not every day will be a success. Setting realistic expectations helps you manage disappointments and stay focused on long-term goals.
3. **Maintain a Long-Term Perspective**: Sales is a marathon, not a sprint. Keep your eye on the bigger picture and remember that consistent effort over time leads to success.
4. **Practice Patience**: Building relationships and closing deals takes time. Be patient and persistent, understanding that each step brings you closer to your goals.
5. **Stay Adaptable**: The sales landscape is constantly evolving. Be open to change and willing to adapt your strategies. Flexibility is key to maintaining resilience in a dynamic environment.

Overcoming Rejection and Failure

Rejection and failure are inevitable in sales. Learning to handle them effectively is crucial for maintaining a winning attitude. Here are strategies to overcome rejection and failure:

1. **Desensitize Yourself to Rejection**: Rejection is part of the process. The more you experience it, the less it will affect you. Treat each rejection as a step closer to a yes.
2. **Separate Yourself from the Outcome**: Remember that rejection is not a reflection of your worth. It's often about the prospect's circumstances or preferences. Stay focused on your efforts and not the immediate outcomes.
3. **Seek Feedback and Improve**: After a rejection or failure, seek feedback to understand what went wrong. Use this information to improve your approach and increase your chances of success next time.
4. **Stay Busy**: Keep your pipeline full and stay active. The more prospects you engage with, the less significant each rejection becomes. Activity breeds confidence and momentum.
5. **Celebrate Small Wins**: Acknowledge and celebrate small victories along the way. This keeps you motivated and reminds you of your progress, even in the face of setbacks.

Continuous Improvement and Learning

A winning attitude is rooted in the commitment to continuous improvement and learning. Here's how to foster a mindset of growth and development:

1. **Invest in Your Education**: Attend workshops, read books, and take courses to enhance your skills and knowledge. The more you learn, the more confident and effective you will become.
2. **Seek Mentorship**: Find mentors who can provide guidance, share experiences, and offer valuable insights. Learning from others accelerates your growth and helps you avoid common pitfalls.

3. **Reflect on Your Experiences**: Regularly take time to reflect on your sales experiences. Identify what worked, what didn't, and how you can improve. This practice sharpens your skills and reinforces a growth mindset.
4. **Stay Updated with Industry Trends**: Keep abreast of the latest trends, technologies, and best practices in your industry. Staying informed ensures you remain competitive and can leverage new opportunities.
5. **Embrace a Growth Mindset**: Believe that your abilities and intelligence can be developed through effort and learning. This mindset fosters resilience, creativity, and a willingness to take on new challenges.

Maintaining Work-Life Balance

A winning attitude is also about maintaining a healthy work-life balance. Here's how to achieve this:

1. **Set Boundaries**: Clearly define your work and personal time. Avoid letting work spill over into your personal life. Setting boundaries helps prevent burnout and ensures you have time to recharge.
2. **Prioritize Self-Care**: Take care of your physical and mental well-being. Regular exercise, healthy eating, and sufficient sleep are crucial for maintaining high energy levels and a positive attitude.
3. **Schedule Downtime**: Make time for hobbies, relaxation, and activities that bring you joy. Downtime is essential for rejuvenation and maintaining a balanced perspective.
4. **Manage Stress**: Develop effective stress management techniques such as meditation, mindfulness, or deep-breathing exercises.

Managing stress is crucial for maintaining a positive and resilient attitude.

5. **Seek Support**: Don't hesitate to seek support from friends, family, or professional counselors when needed. A strong support system helps you navigate challenges and stay motivated.

In summary, building a winning attitude requires a combination of positive mindset, resilience, persistence, continuous improvement, and work-life balance. By cultivating these traits, you will enhance your effectiveness as a sales professional and achieve long-term success. Remember, a winning attitude is not just about achieving your goals but also about enjoying the journey and growing as an individual.

Chapter 4: Prospecting Like a Pro

Prospecting is the lifeblood of sales. It's the process of identifying potential customers who may be interested in your product or service. Effective prospecting can significantly increase your chances of closing deals and achieving your sales targets. In this chapter, we will explore advanced techniques for prospecting like a pro, including identifying your target market, effective lead generation strategies, and leveraging social media and technology.

Identifying Your Target Market

Before you begin prospecting, it's essential to clearly define your target market. Understanding who your ideal customers are will help you focus your efforts and increase your efficiency. Here's how to identify your target market:

1. **Analyze Your Current Customers**: Look at your existing customer base to identify common characteristics such as industry, company size, location, and buying behavior. This analysis can help you create a profile of your ideal customer.
2. **Research Your Competitors**: Study your competitors and identify who their customers are. This can provide insights into potential markets you may have overlooked.
3. **Segment Your Market**: Divide your market into segments based on specific criteria such as demographics, psychographics, and firmographics. This segmentation allows you to tailor your prospecting efforts to each group's unique needs and preferences.
4. **Create Buyer Personas**: Develop detailed buyer personas that represent your ideal customers. Include information such as their job titles, responsibilities, challenges, and goals. Buyer

personas help you understand and connect with your prospects on a deeper level.

Effective Lead Generation Strategies

Generating high-quality leads is a critical aspect of successful prospecting. Here are some effective lead generation strategies:

1. **Content Marketing**: Create valuable content such as blog posts, whitepapers, eBooks, and webinars that address the pain points and interests of your target market. Share this content through your website, social media, and email marketing to attract and engage potential leads.
2. **Networking**: Attend industry events, conferences, and trade shows to meet potential prospects. Networking provides an opportunity to build relationships and establish yourself as a knowledgeable and trusted professional in your field.
3. **Referrals**: Leverage your existing customer base to generate referrals. Satisfied customers are often willing to recommend your product or service to others. Implement a referral program to incentivize and reward customers who refer new business to you.
4. **Cold Calling**: While it may seem old-fashioned, cold calling can still be an effective lead generation technique when done correctly. Research your prospects thoroughly, prepare a compelling pitch, and approach each call with confidence and persistence.
5. **Email Campaigns**: Develop targeted email campaigns to reach potential prospects. Personalize your emails to address the specific needs and interests of each segment. Use compelling subject

lines and clear calls to action to increase your response rates.

Using Social Media and Technology

Social media and technology have revolutionized the way we prospect. Leveraging these tools can enhance your prospecting efforts and help you reach a wider audience. Here's how to use social media and technology effectively:

1. **LinkedIn**: LinkedIn is a powerful platform for B2B prospecting. Use it to connect with potential prospects, join industry groups, and share valuable content. LinkedIn Sales Navigator can help you identify and reach decision-makers in your target market.
2. **Social Listening**: Use social listening tools to monitor conversations and trends related to your industry. This allows you to identify potential prospects who are discussing topics relevant to your product or service.
3. **Customer Relationship Management (CRM) Systems**: Implement a CRM system to manage your prospecting efforts. A CRM helps you track interactions with prospects, manage your pipeline, and automate follow-up activities.
4. **Automation Tools**: Use automation tools to streamline your prospecting process. Tools like email automation, lead scoring, and chatbots can save you time and ensure you stay in touch with your prospects consistently.
5. **Content Sharing Platforms**: Share your content on platforms like SlideShare, Medium, and industry-specific forums. This increases your visibility and positions you as a thought leader in your field.

The Art of the Cold Call

Cold calling is a time-tested prospecting technique that can yield significant results when done correctly. Here are some tips to master the art of the cold call:

1. **Prepare Thoroughly**: Research your prospects before making the call. Understand their business, industry, and potential pain points. This preparation allows you to tailor your pitch and demonstrate your understanding of their needs.
2. **Craft a Compelling Pitch**: Develop a concise and compelling pitch that grabs the prospect's attention within the first few seconds. Focus on the value you can provide and how your product or service can solve their specific problems.
3. **Handle Objections Confidently**: Be prepared to handle objections and questions from prospects. Listen carefully to their concerns, acknowledge them, and provide clear and persuasive responses.
4. **Stay Persistent**: Cold calling requires persistence. Don't get discouraged by rejections. Keep refining your approach, and remember that every "no" brings you closer to a "yes."
5. **Follow Up**: Effective follow-up is crucial for converting cold calls into leads. Schedule follow-up calls or emails to keep the conversation going and move the prospect through your sales funnel.

Mastering the Follow-Up

Following up with prospects is a critical aspect of prospecting. It shows your commitment and keeps you top of mind. Here are some techniques for effective follow-up:

1. **Create a Follow-Up System**: Develop a systematic approach to follow-up. Use your CRM to set reminders and track your interactions with prospects. Consistent follow-up increases your

chances of building a relationship and closing the deal.

2. **Personalize Your Follow-Up**: Tailor your follow-up messages to each prospect's specific needs and interests. Personalization shows that you value their business and have taken the time to understand their situation.

3. **Provide Value**: Each follow-up should provide additional value. Share relevant content, industry insights, or updates about your product or service. Providing value keeps prospects engaged and positions you as a helpful resource.

4. **Be Persistent but Respectful**: Persistence is key in follow-up, but it's important to respect the prospect's time and preferences. Space out your follow-up messages appropriately and avoid being overly aggressive.

5. **Know When to Move On**: Not every prospect will convert into a customer. Know when to move on and focus your efforts on more promising leads. However, keep the door open for future opportunities by maintaining a positive and professional relationship.

In conclusion, prospecting like a pro involves a combination of identifying your target market, employing effective lead generation strategies, leveraging social media and technology, mastering cold calling, and following up effectively. By honing these skills and consistently applying them, you will build a robust pipeline of high-quality leads and increase your chances of sales success. Remember, prospecting is an ongoing process that requires dedication, persistence, and continuous improvement.

Chapter 5: The Art of the Cold Call

Cold calling is one of the most challenging yet rewarding aspects of sales. It involves contacting potential customers who have not previously expressed interest in your product or service. While it may seem daunting, mastering the art of the cold call can significantly boost your sales pipeline and close rates. In this chapter, we will delve deeply into the nuances of cold calling, from preparation and crafting your pitch to handling objections and closing the deal.

Preparing for Cold Calls

Preparation is crucial for successful cold calling. It sets the stage for a productive conversation and increases your confidence. Here's how to prepare effectively:

1. **Research Your Prospects**: Before picking up the phone, research your prospects thoroughly. Understand their business, industry, and potential pain points. Use tools like LinkedIn, company websites, and industry reports to gather valuable insights.
2. **Create a Call List**: Organize your prospects into a call list. Prioritize them based on factors such as their likelihood to buy, company size, and industry relevance. This helps you focus your efforts on high-potential leads.
3. **Set Clear Objectives**: Define what you want to achieve with each call. Whether it's scheduling a meeting, gathering information, or making a sale, having clear objectives keeps you focused and increases your chances of success.
4. **Develop a Call Script**: While you don't need to follow a script word-for-word, having a structured outline can guide your conversation. Your script

should include an engaging introduction, key points about your product or service, and common objections with responses.

5. **Prepare Your Environment**: Ensure you have a quiet, distraction-free environment for making calls. Have all necessary materials, such as your script, prospect information, and notepad, readily available.

Crafting a Compelling Pitch

Your pitch is the cornerstone of your cold call. It needs to capture the prospect's attention quickly and convey the value of your offering. Here's how to craft a compelling pitch:

1. **Grab Attention Immediately**: The first few seconds of your call are critical. Start with a friendly greeting and a strong opening line that piques the prospect's interest. Avoid generic introductions and get straight to the point.
   Example: "Hi [Prospect's Name], this is [Your Name] from [Your Company]. I noticed your company recently expanded into [New Market], and I wanted to share how we've helped similar businesses streamline their operations during growth."

2. **State Your Purpose Clearly**: Be clear about why you are calling and what you hope to achieve. This sets the tone for the conversation and shows respect for the prospect's time.
   Example: "I'm reaching out to see if we might be able to help you improve [specific aspect of their business], just as we've done for other companies in your industry."

3. **Highlight Key Benefits**: Focus on the benefits of your product or service, rather than just its features. Explain how it can solve the prospect's pain points

or improve their business.

Example: "Our solution helps companies like yours reduce [specific problem] by [percentage] and increase [specific benefit] by [percentage]."

4. **Engage with a Question**: Asking an open-ended question encourages the prospect to engage in the conversation and provides you with valuable information.

Example: "Can you share how you currently handle [specific process] and any challenges you're facing?"

Handling Objections and Staying Persistent

Objections are a natural part of cold calling. How you handle them can determine the success of your call. Here are strategies for addressing common objections:

1. **Listen Actively**: When a prospect raises an objection, listen carefully without interrupting. This shows respect and helps you understand their concerns fully.

2. **Acknowledge and Empathize**: Acknowledge the prospect's concerns and empathize with their situation. This builds rapport and demonstrates that you value their perspective.

Example: "I understand that budget constraints are a concern for many companies, especially in today's economy."

3. **Address the Objection Directly**: Provide a clear and concise response to the objection. Use facts, testimonials, and case studies to support your points.

Example: "While our solution requires an initial investment, many of our clients find that it pays for itself within the first six months by reducing operational costs and increasing efficiency."

4. **Ask Clarifying Questions**: Sometimes, objections are based on misunderstandings or lack of information. Ask clarifying questions to get to the root of the concern.
    Example: "Can you tell me more about what specifically worries you about the implementation process?"

5. **Reiterate Benefits**: Circle back to the benefits of your product or service. Remind the prospect how it addresses their pain points and improves their situation.
    Example: "Our solution not only addresses your current challenges but also positions your company for future growth by [specific benefit]."

6. **Stay Persistent**: Persistence is key in cold calling. Don't get discouraged by initial rejections. Follow up with prospects, provide additional information, and keep the conversation going.
    Example: "I understand this might not be the best time. Would it be okay if I followed up with you next month to see if your situation has changed?"

Chapter 6: Mastering the Follow-Up

Mastering the follow-up is essential for turning prospects into customers. A well-executed follow-up strategy demonstrates your commitment, keeps you top of mind, and helps build a relationship with your prospects. In this chapter, we will explore techniques for effective follow-up, including creating a follow-up system, personalizing your follow-up, providing value, maintaining persistence, and knowing when to move on.

The Importance of Follow-Up

The follow-up is a critical part of the sales process. Research shows that most sales are made after multiple follow-up attempts. However, many salespeople give up too soon. Here are some key reasons why follow-up is important:

1. **Builds Relationships**: Regular follow-up helps you build a relationship with your prospects. It shows that you care about their needs and are committed to helping them.
2. **Keeps You Top of Mind**: Regular contact ensures that you stay top of mind with your prospects. When they are ready to make a purchase, they will think of you first.
3. **Demonstrates Persistence**: Persistence is a key trait of successful salespeople. Regular follow-up shows that you are serious about helping your prospects and willing to go the extra mile.
4. **Provides Opportunities for Additional Information**: Follow-up allows you to provide additional information and address any concerns or objections that the prospect may have.
5. **Increases Your Chances of Closing**: The more touchpoints you have with a prospect, the higher your chances of closing the deal. Each follow-up is

an opportunity to move the prospect closer to a decision.

Creating a Follow-Up System

Having a systematic approach to follow-up ensures that no prospect falls through the cracks. Here's how to create an effective follow-up system:

1. **Use a CRM System**: A Customer Relationship Management (CRM) system helps you track your interactions with prospects, schedule follow-ups, and set reminders. It ensures that you stay organized and can manage your follow-up activities efficiently.
2. **Segment Your Prospects**: Divide your prospects into different segments based on their stage in the sales funnel, level of interest, and potential value. This helps you tailor your follow-up approach to each segment's unique needs.
3. **Set Follow-Up Goals**: Define clear goals for each follow-up. Whether it's scheduling a meeting, providing additional information, or addressing a specific objection, having clear goals keeps your follow-up focused and effective.
4. **Develop a Follow-Up Schedule**: Create a follow-up schedule that outlines when and how often you will contact your prospects. Be consistent with your follow-up efforts to maintain momentum and build a relationship.
5. **Track Your Progress**: Regularly review your follow-up activities and track your progress. Identify what's working and what's not, and adjust your approach as needed.

Personalizing Your Follow-Up

Personalization is key to effective follow-up. Tailoring your messages to each prospect's specific needs and interests shows that you value their business and have taken the time to understand their situation. Here's how to personalize your follow-up:

1. **Reference Previous Conversations**: Mention details from your previous interactions to show that you remember and value the prospect's input. This helps build rapport and trust.
   Example: "Hi [Prospect's Name], following up on our conversation last week about your current challenges with [specific issue]..."
2. **Use the Prospect's Name**: Addressing the prospect by their name makes your communication more personal and engaging.
3. **Tailor Your Message**: Customize your message to address the prospect's specific needs and pain points. Highlight how your product or service can help them achieve their goals.
   Example: "Based on what you shared about your need to improve [specific process], I wanted to provide some additional information on how our solution can help..."
4. **Provide Relevant Content**: Share content that is relevant to the prospect's industry, role, or specific challenges. This adds value to your follow-up and positions you as a helpful resource.
   Example: "I came across this article about [relevant topic] and thought it might be of interest to you..."
5. **Be Authentic**: Authenticity is important in building trust. Be genuine in your communication and show that you genuinely care about helping the prospect.

Providing Value in Every Interaction

Each follow-up should provide additional value to the prospect. This keeps them engaged and interested in your solution. Here's how to provide value in every interaction:

1. **Share Insights and Best Practices**: Provide insights and best practices related to the prospect's industry or specific challenges. This positions you as an expert and adds value to your follow-up.
   Example: "I wanted to share some best practices for improving [specific process] that we've seen work well for other companies in your industry..."

2. **Offer Solutions to Their Problems**: Address the prospect's pain points and offer solutions that can help them overcome their challenges.
   Example: "I understand that [specific issue] is a challenge for you. Here's how our solution can help you address this issue..."

3. **Provide Case Studies and Testimonials**: Share case studies and testimonials from similar clients who have benefited from your product or service. This builds credibility and demonstrates the value of your solution.
   Example: "I thought you might be interested in this case study about how we helped [similar company] achieve [specific result]..."

4. **Invite Them to Events or Webinars**: Invite prospects to events, webinars, or workshops that are relevant to their interests and needs. This provides value and keeps them engaged with your brand.
   Example: "We're hosting a webinar on [relevant topic] next week, and I thought it might be of interest to you. Here are the details..."

5. **Offer a Free Trial or Demo**: Offering a free trial or demo allows prospects to experience the value of your product or service firsthand.
   Example: "I'd like to offer you a free trial of our solution so you can see how it can benefit your

business. Let me know if you're interested, and I'll set it up for you."

Being Persistent but Respectful

Persistence is key to successful follow-up, but it's important to be respectful of the prospect's time and preferences. Here's how to strike the right balance:

1. **Space Out Your Follow-Ups**: Avoid overwhelming the prospect with too many follow-ups in a short period. Space out your follow-ups appropriately to give them time to consider your offer.
2. **Vary Your Follow-Up Methods**: Use different methods to follow up, such as phone calls, emails, and social media messages. This keeps your follow-up efforts fresh and less intrusive.
3. **Respect Their Preferences**: Pay attention to the prospect's communication preferences and tailor your follow-up accordingly. If they prefer email over phone calls, respect that preference.
4. **Be Polite and Professional**: Always maintain a polite and professional tone in your follow-up messages. Thank the prospect for their time and express your willingness to assist them.
    Example: "Thank you for taking the time to speak with me last week. I'm here to answer any questions you may have and provide any additional information you need."
5. **Know When to Back Off**: If a prospect consistently shows no interest or asks you to stop contacting them, respect their wishes and back off. However, keep the door open for future opportunities.
    Example: "I understand that now may not be the right time. If your situation changes or if you have

any questions in the future, please don't hesitate to reach out."

Knowing When to Move On

Not every prospect will convert into a customer. It's important to know when to move on and focus your efforts on more promising leads. Here's how to identify when it's time to move on:

1. **Lack of Response**: If a prospect consistently does not respond to your follow-up attempts after multiple tries, it may be time to move on. Keep track of your attempts and set a limit for how many follow-ups you will make.
2. **Consistent Rejection**: If a prospect consistently rejects your offers and shows no interest in your solution, it may be time to move on. However, keep the door open for future opportunities by maintaining a positive and professional relationship.
3. **No Fit**: If you determine that your product or service is not a good fit for the prospect's needs, it's best to move on and focus on more suitable leads.
4. **Referral Opportunities**: Even if a prospect is not interested, they may know someone who could benefit from your solution. Politely ask for referrals and express your willingness to help their network. Example: "I understand that our solution may not be the right fit for you at this time. If you know anyone else who might benefit, I would appreciate any referrals."
5. **Review and Adjust**: Regularly review your follow-up process and adjust your approach as needed. Identify patterns and areas for improvement to enhance your follow-up strategy.

Conclusion

Mastering the follow-up is crucial for sales success. By creating a systematic approach, personalizing your messages, providing value, being persistent yet respectful, and knowing when to move on, you can build strong relationships with your prospects and increase your chances of closing deals. Remember, follow-up is not just about closing the sale; it's about building trust and demonstrating your commitment to helping your prospects achieve their goals. By consistently applying these strategies, you will become a master of the follow-up and a more successful sales professional.

Chapter 7: Presenting with Confidence

Presenting with confidence is an essential skill for any salesperson. A confident presentation not only conveys your message effectively but also builds trust and credibility with your audience. In this chapter, we will explore how to craft compelling presentations, engage your audience, and use stories and visuals to enhance your delivery.

Crafting Compelling Presentations

A compelling presentation is well-structured, clear, and focused on delivering value to your audience. Here's how to craft a presentation that captivates and persuades:

1. **Understand Your Audience**: Before you start crafting your presentation, it's crucial to understand your audience. Know their needs, interests, and pain points. Tailor your message to address these specific aspects.
2. **Define Your Key Message**: What is the main point you want your audience to remember? Define a clear and concise key message that will resonate with your audience. Ensure that all parts of your presentation support this key message.
3. **Create a Logical Flow**: Structure your presentation with a clear beginning, middle, and end. Start with an engaging introduction, followed by the main content, and conclude with a strong closing. Each section should flow logically into the next.
4. **Keep It Simple**: Avoid overwhelming your audience with too much information. Focus on the most important points and present them clearly. Use simple language and avoid jargon.
5. **Highlight Benefits**: Emphasize the benefits of your product or service. Explain how it can solve your

audience's problems or improve their situation. Highlight the value it brings to them.

6. **Use Supporting Data**: Include relevant data, statistics, and case studies to support your points. This adds credibility to your presentation and helps persuade your audience.

7. **Prepare for Questions**: Anticipate potential questions and objections from your audience. Prepare clear and concise answers to address them confidently.

Engaging Your Audience

Engaging your audience is key to delivering a successful presentation. Here are strategies to capture and maintain their attention:

1. **Start with a Hook**: Begin your presentation with a compelling hook that grabs your audience's attention. This could be a surprising fact, a relevant story, or a thought-provoking question.

2. **Make Eye Contact**: Eye contact helps build a connection with your audience. It shows that you are confident and engaged with them. Make sure to look at different members of the audience throughout your presentation.

3. **Use Body Language**: Your body language plays a significant role in how your message is received. Stand tall, use open gestures, and move naturally. Avoid crossing your arms or hiding behind a podium.

4. **Vary Your Voice**: Use variations in your tone, pitch, and volume to keep your audience engaged. Emphasize key points with a louder or softer voice, and use pauses for impact.

5. **Involve Your Audience**: Encourage audience participation by asking questions, inviting

comments, or conducting polls. This makes your presentation interactive and keeps the audience engaged.

6. **Be Enthusiastic**: Show enthusiasm for your topic. Your energy and passion will be contagious and help keep your audience interested.

7. **Handle Distractions Gracefully**: If you encounter distractions, handle them gracefully. Stay focused, address the issue calmly, and quickly return to your presentation.

Using Stories and Visuals

Stories and visuals are powerful tools for making your presentation more engaging and memorable. Here's how to effectively incorporate them into your presentation:

1. **Tell Relevant Stories**: Use stories that are relevant to your audience and illustrate your key points. Stories make your message more relatable and easier to remember.
   Example: "Let me tell you about one of our clients, Jane, who faced a similar challenge. She was struggling with [specific issue], but after using our solution, she saw a [specific result]."

2. **Use Visual Aids**: Visual aids such as slides, videos, and infographics can enhance your presentation and help convey your message more effectively. Use visuals to highlight key points, illustrate data, and provide visual interest.

3. **Keep Slides Simple**: When using slides, keep them simple and uncluttered. Use bullet points, short phrases, and clear images. Avoid overloading slides with text.

4. **Highlight Key Data**: Use charts, graphs, and infographics to present data in a visually appealing

way. Highlight the most important data points and explain their significance.

5. **Use High-Quality Images**: Use high-quality images that are relevant to your content. Avoid using generic stock photos. Authentic images that relate to your message are more effective.

6. **Incorporate Videos**: Videos can be a powerful way to illustrate your points and keep your audience engaged. Use short, relevant videos that enhance your message.

7. **Practice Timing**: Practice your presentation to ensure that your use of stories and visuals is well-timed and seamless. Avoid spending too much time on any one slide or story.

Tips for Presenting with Confidence

Confidence in presenting comes from preparation and practice. Here are some tips to help you present with confidence:

1. **Practice, Practice, Practice**: The more you practice, the more confident you will be. Rehearse your presentation multiple times, both alone and in front of others. Practice helps you become familiar with your material and improves your delivery.

2. **Know Your Material**: Be thoroughly familiar with your content. Knowing your material inside and out allows you to present more naturally and respond confidently to questions.

3. **Visualize Success**: Before your presentation, take a few moments to visualize yourself delivering a successful presentation. Imagine yourself speaking confidently, engaging your audience, and achieving your goals.

4. **Manage Nervousness**: It's normal to feel nervous before a presentation. Use deep-breathing techniques, positive affirmations, and visualization

to calm your nerves. Focus on your message and the value you are providing to your audience.

5. **Start Strong**: A strong start sets the tone for your presentation. Begin with a confident greeting, an engaging hook, and a clear statement of your purpose. This helps you establish control and capture your audience's attention.

6. **Stay Positive**: Maintain a positive attitude throughout your presentation. If you make a mistake, don't dwell on it. Correct it if necessary and move on confidently.

7. **Seek Feedback**: After your presentation, seek feedback from colleagues or mentors. Constructive feedback helps you identify areas for improvement and build your confidence for future presentations.

Conclusion

Presenting with confidence is a skill that can be developed with practice and preparation. By crafting compelling presentations, engaging your audience, and using stories and visuals effectively, you can deliver presentations that captivate and persuade. Remember, confidence comes from knowing your material, understanding your audience, and believing in the value of your message. With these techniques, you will be able to present with confidence and achieve your sales goals.

Chapter 8: Closing the Deal

Closing the deal is the final and most critical step in the sales process. It requires recognizing buying signals, employing effective closing techniques and strategies, and handling last-minute objections with confidence. In this chapter, we will delve into these key aspects to help you close deals successfully and consistently.

Recognizing Buying Signals

Recognizing buying signals is essential for knowing when to move toward closing the deal. Buying signals are verbal and non-verbal cues that indicate a prospect's readiness to make a purchase. Here are common buying signals to watch for:

1. **Positive Body Language**: Leaning forward, nodding, and maintaining eye contact are signs of interest. A prospect who is engaged physically is likely engaged mentally as well.
2. **Questions About Implementation**: When a prospect starts asking detailed questions about how your product or service works, delivery times, or implementation processes, it indicates a strong interest.
   Example: "How soon can we get this up and running?"
3. **Expressions of Agreement**: Verbal affirmations such as "That makes sense," "I like that," or "Exactly what we need" show that the prospect is aligning with your presentation.
4. **Ownership Language**: When prospects start referring to your product or service as if it is already theirs, it's a clear buying signal.
   Example: "Once we have this in place, we can..."

5. **Budget Questions**: Inquiries about pricing, payment terms, and budget allocation suggest that the prospect is seriously considering making a purchase.
6. **Decision-Maker Involvement**: If a prospect brings other decision-makers into the conversation, it indicates that they are moving closer to a buying decision.
7. **Trial Closes**: Prospects might give indirect trial closes by asking about guarantees, return policies, or after-sales service.

Closing Techniques and Strategies

There are various closing techniques and strategies you can use to seal the deal. The key is to choose the right one based on the situation and the prospect's behavior. Here are some effective closing techniques:

1. **The Assumptive Close**: Act as if the prospect has already decided to purchase and proceed with the next steps.
   Example: "Great, I'll schedule the delivery for next Monday."
2. **The Direct Close**: Ask for the sale directly and confidently. This straightforward approach can be very effective.
   Example: "Are you ready to move forward with this purchase?"
3. **The Summary Close**: Summarize the key benefits and value of your product or service, then ask for the sale.
   Example: "So, to recap, our solution will improve your efficiency by 30%, reduce costs by 20%, and provide a dedicated support team. Shall we go ahead and get started?"

4. **The Option Close**: Give the prospect a choice between two positive options, both of which lead to a close.
Example: "Would you prefer the standard package or the premium package?"

5. **The Urgency Close**: Create a sense of urgency to encourage the prospect to make a decision quickly.
Example: "We have a special offer that ends this Friday. Can I reserve this for you today?"

6. **The Balance Sheet Close**: List the pros and cons of your product or service, with the pros outweighing the cons, to help the prospect make a decision.
Example: "Let's weigh the benefits: increased productivity, cost savings, and excellent support. The only con is the initial setup time, which we will assist you with. What do you think?"

7. **The Columbo Close**: Named after the famous TV detective, this technique involves asking a seemingly offhand question just as you're about to leave, which brings the conversation back to closing.
Example: "Just one more thing—what's holding you back from making a decision today?"

Handling Last-Minute Objections

Handling last-minute objections is crucial for closing the deal. Prospects often raise objections as they get closer to making a decision. Here's how to address them effectively:

1. **Listen Actively**: Give the prospect your full attention and listen to their objection without interrupting. This shows respect and helps you understand their concern fully.

2. **Acknowledge the Objection**: Validate the prospect's concern to show that you understand and respect their viewpoint.

Example: "I understand that the upfront cost is a concern for you."

3. **Ask Clarifying Questions**: Get to the root of the objection by asking questions that clarify the prospect's concerns.
Example: "Can you tell me more about why the initial cost is a concern for you?"

4. **Provide Reassurance**: Address the objection with reassurance and evidence. Use testimonials, case studies, and data to support your response.
Example: "Many of our clients had the same concern initially. However, they found that the cost savings and increased efficiency they achieved within the first few months more than justified the investment. Here's a case study that illustrates this..."

5. **Reframe the Objection**: Turn the objection into a positive by reframing it in a way that highlights the benefits of your product or service.
Example: "I see the initial cost as an investment that will lead to significant long-term savings and improved performance for your team."

6. **Trial Close**: Use a trial close to gauge if you have successfully addressed the objection and if the prospect is ready to move forward.
Example: "Does that address your concern about the cost? Can we proceed with the next steps?"

7. **Stay Calm and Confident**: Maintain your composure and confidence throughout the conversation. Your attitude can influence the prospect's perception and decision.

Conclusion

Closing the deal is a critical skill that requires recognizing buying signals, employing effective closing techniques, and handling last-minute objections with confidence. By mastering these aspects, you can increase your close rates and achieve greater sales success. Remember, closing is not about pressuring the prospect but about guiding them to make a decision that benefits both parties. With practice and persistence, you will become adept at closing deals and building lasting relationships with your clients.

Chapter 9: Time Management for Sales Professionals

Effective time management is essential for sales professionals. Balancing multiple tasks, meetings, and follow-ups requires a strategic approach to ensure productivity and success. In this chapter, we will explore prioritizing tasks, time-blocking techniques, and strategies for maximizing productivity.

Prioritizing Your Tasks

Prioritizing tasks helps you focus on what's most important and ensures that you spend your time on activities that drive the most value. Here's how to prioritize effectively:

1. **Identify Key Tasks**: List all the tasks you need to accomplish. Include daily, weekly, and long-term tasks. Categorize them based on urgency and importance.
2. **Use the Eisenhower Matrix**: The Eisenhower Matrix, also known as the Urgent-Important Matrix, helps you categorize tasks into four quadrants:
   - **Urgent and Important**: Tasks that require immediate attention (e.g., closing deals, urgent client requests).
   - **Important but Not Urgent**: Tasks that are important but can be scheduled (e.g., planning, relationship building).
   - **Urgent but Not Important**: Tasks that need to be done quickly but are less critical (e.g., minor administrative tasks).
   - **Not Urgent and Not Important**: Tasks that can be delegated or eliminated (e.g., low-value activities).

1. **Set SMART Goals**: Ensure your goals are Specific, Measurable, Achievable, Relevant, and Time-bound. This helps you stay focused and measure your progress.
2. **Prioritize High-Value Activities**: Focus on tasks that directly impact your sales goals, such as prospecting, client meetings, and follow-ups. Allocate more time to these high-value activities.
3. **Plan Your Day the Night Before**: Review your task list and prioritize tasks for the next day. This helps you start your day with a clear plan and reduces decision fatigue.
4. **Avoid Multitasking**: Multitasking can reduce productivity and increase errors. Focus on one task at a time to ensure high-quality work and efficiency.

Time Blocking Techniques

Time blocking is a powerful technique that involves dividing your day into blocks of time dedicated to specific tasks. Here's how to implement time blocking effectively:

1. **Create a Daily Schedule**: Divide your day into blocks of time dedicated to different tasks. For example, allocate specific times for prospecting, meetings, follow-ups, and administrative work.
2. **Prioritize High-Impact Activities**: Schedule your most important and high-impact activities during your peak productivity hours. For many people, this is in the morning.
3. **Set Boundaries**: Allocate specific time blocks for tasks and stick to them. Avoid letting less important tasks spill over into time blocks dedicated to high-priority activities.
4. **Include Buffer Time**: Schedule buffer time between tasks to account for unexpected delays or

additional tasks. This helps you stay on track without feeling overwhelmed.

5. **Use Technology**: Utilize calendar tools and time management apps to plan and manage your time blocks. Set reminders to stay on schedule and track your progress.

6. **Review and Adjust**: At the end of each day, review your time blocks and assess your productivity. Adjust your schedule as needed to improve efficiency and effectiveness.

Maximizing Productivity

Maximizing productivity involves optimizing your work habits and environment to achieve more in less time. Here are strategies to boost your productivity:

1. **Minimize Distractions**: Identify and eliminate distractions in your work environment. This includes turning off non-essential notifications, setting boundaries with colleagues, and creating a dedicated workspace.

2. **Use the Pomodoro Technique**: The Pomodoro Technique involves working in focused intervals, typically 25 minutes, followed by a short break. This helps maintain concentration and prevent burnout.

3. **Delegate and Automate**: Delegate tasks that can be handled by others and automate repetitive tasks using tools and software. This frees up your time for high-value activities.

4. **Practice the Two-Minute Rule**: If a task can be completed in two minutes or less, do it immediately. This prevents small tasks from piling up and becoming overwhelming.

5. **Take Regular Breaks**: Schedule regular breaks to rest and recharge. Short breaks throughout the day can improve focus and productivity.
6. **Stay Organized**: Keep your workspace and digital files organized. Use tools like to-do lists, project management software, and filing systems to stay organized and on top of your tasks.
7. **Reflect and Improve**: Regularly reflect on your work habits and productivity. Identify areas for improvement and implement changes to enhance your efficiency.
8. **Focus on Continuous Learning**: Invest in your personal and professional development. Attend workshops, read books, and seek feedback to continuously improve your skills and knowledge.

Conclusion

Effective time management is crucial for sales professionals to achieve their goals and maximize productivity. By prioritizing tasks, implementing time-blocking techniques, and adopting strategies to boost productivity, you can make the most of your time and drive greater success in your sales career. Remember, time management is not just about working harder but about working smarter and making intentional choices to achieve your objectives.

Chapter 10: Leveraging Technology and Tools

In today's fast-paced sales environment, leveraging technology and tools is crucial for gaining a competitive edge. Effective use of technology can streamline your sales processes, improve efficiency, and provide valuable insights to drive better decision-making. In this chapter, we will explore the benefits of CRM systems, sales automation tools, and data-driven sales strategies.

CRM Systems

Customer Relationship Management (CRM) systems are essential tools for managing your interactions with current and potential customers. Here's how CRM systems can benefit your sales efforts:

1. **Centralized Data Management**: CRM systems store all customer information in one place, making it easy to access and update. This ensures that you have a complete view of each customer's history and interactions with your company.
2. **Improved Customer Relationships**: By tracking customer interactions and preferences, CRM systems help you provide personalized service and build stronger relationships. You can tailor your communications and offers based on individual customer needs and behaviors.
3. **Sales Pipeline Management**: CRM systems allow you to track the status of each deal in your sales pipeline. This helps you identify bottlenecks, prioritize opportunities, and forecast sales more accurately.
4. **Automation of Routine Tasks**: CRM systems can automate routine tasks such as follow-up emails, appointment scheduling, and data entry. This frees

up your time to focus on high-value activities like prospecting and closing deals.

5. **Enhanced Collaboration**: CRM systems facilitate collaboration among team members by providing a shared platform for managing customer information and sales activities. This ensures that everyone is on the same page and can work together effectively.

6. **Reporting and Analytics**: CRM systems offer robust reporting and analytics capabilities. You can generate reports on various metrics such as sales performance, customer behavior, and campaign effectiveness. These insights help you make data-driven decisions and continuously improve your sales strategies.

Sales Automation Tools

Sales automation tools streamline repetitive tasks, improve efficiency, and enhance the overall sales process. Here's how to leverage sales automation tools effectively:

1. **Automated Email Campaigns**: Use sales automation tools to create and send targeted email campaigns. Segment your audience based on criteria such as industry, job role, and behavior, and send personalized messages that resonate with each segment.

2. **Lead Scoring and Qualification**: Automate lead scoring and qualification to prioritize high-potential leads. Sales automation tools can assign scores based on criteria such as engagement level, company size, and decision-making authority, helping you focus your efforts on the most promising prospects.

3. **Follow-Up Reminders**: Set up automated reminders for follow-ups to ensure that no lead falls through the cracks. This helps you stay organized

and maintain consistent communication with prospects.

4. **Appointment Scheduling**: Use automation tools to streamline appointment scheduling. Prospects can book meetings directly through your calendar, reducing the back-and-forth emails and ensuring that your schedule is always up-to-date.

5. **Sales Proposals and Quotes**: Automate the creation and delivery of sales proposals and quotes. This ensures that your documents are accurate, professional, and sent in a timely manner.

6. **Task Management**: Sales automation tools can help you manage and track tasks related to each deal. This ensures that you stay on top of deadlines and follow through on commitments.

Data-Driven Sales Strategies

Data-driven sales strategies leverage data and analytics to make informed decisions and optimize the sales process. Here's how to implement data-driven sales strategies:

1. **Collect and Analyze Data**: Collect data from various sources such as CRM systems, website analytics, and marketing automation tools. Analyze this data to gain insights into customer behavior, preferences, and pain points.

2. **Identify Patterns and Trends**: Look for patterns and trends in your data that can inform your sales strategies. For example, identify which types of content resonate most with your audience, which marketing channels generate the most leads, and which sales tactics are most effective.

3. **Personalize Your Approach**: Use data to personalize your sales approach. Tailor your messaging, offers, and communications based on individual customer preferences and behaviors.

Personalized interactions are more likely to engage prospects and drive conversions.

4. **Optimize Sales Processes**: Continuously analyze your sales processes to identify areas for improvement. Use data to track the effectiveness of different sales tactics, optimize your sales funnel, and reduce friction points.

5. **Measure and Adjust**: Regularly measure the performance of your sales strategies using key metrics such as conversion rates, customer acquisition costs, and lifetime value. Adjust your strategies based on these insights to continuously improve your results.

6. **Predictive Analytics**: Leverage predictive analytics to forecast future sales and identify potential opportunities. Predictive models can help you anticipate customer needs, identify high-value prospects, and allocate resources more effectively.

Conclusion

Leveraging technology and tools is essential for modern sales professionals. CRM systems, sales automation tools, and data-driven sales strategies can streamline your processes, improve efficiency, and provide valuable insights to drive better decision-making. By effectively utilizing these technologies, you can enhance your sales performance, build stronger customer relationships, and achieve greater success in your sales career. Remember, the key to leveraging technology is to continuously evaluate and optimize your approach based on data and insights.

Chapter 11: Continuous Improvement and Learning

Continuous improvement and learning are essential for long-term success in sales. The landscape of sales is constantly evolving, and staying ahead requires a commitment to ongoing development. In this chapter, we will explore strategies for staying updated with industry trends, investing in personal development, and learning from every experience.

Staying Updated with Industry Trends

Keeping up with industry trends ensures that you remain relevant and competitive in your field. Here are some strategies for staying updated:

1. **Follow Industry Publications and Blogs**: Subscribe to industry-specific magazines, journals, and blogs. These publications provide insights into the latest trends, technologies, and best practices.
2. **Join Professional Associations**: Become a member of professional associations related to your industry. These organizations often provide valuable resources, networking opportunities, and updates on industry developments.
3. **Attend Conferences and Trade Shows**: Participate in industry conferences, trade shows, and seminars. These events offer opportunities to learn from experts, discover new products and services, and network with peers.
4. **Network with Peers**: Engage with other professionals in your industry through networking events, online forums, and social media groups. Sharing experiences and insights with peers can provide valuable perspectives and keep you informed about the latest trends.

5. **Subscribe to Newsletters**: Sign up for newsletters from industry leaders, companies, and thought leaders. Newsletters often highlight recent developments, case studies, and success stories.
6. **Leverage Social Media**: Follow industry influencers, companies, and organizations on social media platforms like LinkedIn, Twitter, and Facebook. Social media is a great way to stay updated with real-time information and engage in relevant discussions.

Investing in Personal Development

Investing in personal development is crucial for enhancing your skills and advancing your career. Here's how to invest in your personal growth:

1. **Take Courses and Certifications**: Enroll in courses and certification programs to gain new skills and knowledge. Many online platforms offer courses on sales techniques, leadership, communication, and other relevant topics.
2. **Read Books**: Reading books on sales, personal development, and leadership can provide valuable insights and inspiration. Make it a habit to read regularly and apply the concepts you learn.
3. **Attend Workshops and Seminars**: Participate in workshops and seminars to learn from experts and engage in hands-on activities. These events often provide practical skills and strategies that you can implement immediately.
4. **Find a Mentor**: Seek out a mentor who can provide guidance, feedback, and support. A mentor can help you navigate challenges, set goals, and accelerate your growth.
5. **Set Personal Development Goals**: Define clear personal development goals and create a plan to

achieve them. Regularly review your progress and adjust your plan as needed.

6. **Practice Self-Reflection**: Regularly reflect on your experiences, strengths, and areas for improvement. Self-reflection helps you gain a deeper understanding of yourself and identify opportunities for growth.

Learning from Every Experience

Every experience, whether positive or negative, provides an opportunity to learn and grow. Here's how to maximize learning from your experiences:

1. **Analyze Successes and Failures**: Take time to analyze both your successes and failures. Identify what worked well and what didn't, and understand the reasons behind the outcomes. Use these insights to improve your strategies and approach.

2. **Seek Feedback**: Actively seek feedback from colleagues, clients, and supervisors. Constructive feedback helps you understand different perspectives and identify areas for improvement.

3. **Document Lessons Learned**: Keep a journal or log of lessons learned from your experiences. Documenting these lessons helps you remember key insights and apply them in the future.

4. **Embrace a Growth Mindset**: Adopt a growth mindset, which is the belief that your abilities and intelligence can be developed through effort and learning. This mindset encourages you to view challenges as opportunities for growth and to persist in the face of setbacks.

5. **Experiment and Innovate**: Don't be afraid to experiment with new approaches and strategies. Innovation often comes from trying new things and

learning from the results. Be open to change and willing to adapt.

6. **Learn from Others**: Observe and learn from the experiences of others. Study successful sales professionals, leaders, and organizations. Analyze their strategies and practices to understand what makes them successful.

Conclusion

Continuous improvement and learning are vital for sustained success in sales. By staying updated with industry trends, investing in personal development, and learning from every experience, you can enhance your skills, stay competitive, and achieve your career goals. Remember, the journey of improvement is ongoing, and the commitment to learning and growth will set you apart as a top-performing sales professional. Embrace the mindset of continuous improvement, and you will continually evolve and thrive in your sales career.

Chapter 12: Maintaining Work-Life Balance

Maintaining a healthy work-life balance is essential for long-term success and well-being in sales. The demands of a sales career can be intense, making it crucial to manage stress, prevent burnout, and integrate work and personal life effectively. In this chapter, we will explore strategies for managing stress and burnout, achieving work-life integration, and prioritizing self-care.

Managing Stress and Burnout

Stress and burnout are common challenges in the sales profession. Here's how to manage them effectively:

1. **Recognize the Signs of Burnout**: Early signs of burnout include feeling exhausted, disengaged, and less effective at work. Pay attention to these signs and take action before burnout becomes severe.
2. **Set Realistic Goals**: Set achievable goals and manage your expectations. Unrealistic goals can lead to stress and disappointment. Break larger goals into smaller, manageable tasks.
3. **Prioritize Tasks**: Use prioritization techniques to focus on high-impact activities. This helps you manage your workload more effectively and reduces feelings of being overwhelmed.
4. **Delegate When Possible**: Don't hesitate to delegate tasks to colleagues or team members. Delegating can lighten your load and allow you to focus on more critical tasks.
5. **Take Breaks**: Regular breaks throughout the day can help reduce stress and increase productivity. Use techniques like the Pomodoro Technique to schedule short breaks after periods of focused work.
6. **Practice Mindfulness**: Mindfulness techniques, such as meditation and deep-breathing exercises,

can help manage stress. Take a few minutes each day to practice mindfulness and clear your mind.

7. **Seek Support**: Don't hesitate to seek support from colleagues, supervisors, or a professional counselor. Sharing your concerns and seeking advice can provide relief and new perspectives.

Strategies for Work-Life Integration

Work-life integration involves blending work and personal life in a way that allows you to thrive in both areas. Here are strategies for achieving effective work-life integration:

1. **Set Boundaries**: Clearly define your work and personal time. Set boundaries to ensure that work does not encroach on your personal life. Communicate these boundaries to your colleagues and family.

2. **Create a Flexible Schedule**: Whenever possible, create a flexible work schedule that accommodates your personal life. Flexibility can reduce stress and help you manage personal responsibilities.

3. **Use Technology Wisely**: Leverage technology to work more efficiently, but also know when to disconnect. Avoid checking work emails or messages during personal time to maintain a healthy balance.

4. **Plan Personal Time**: Schedule personal activities and family time just as you would schedule work tasks. Planning personal time ensures that you make time for the activities that bring you joy and relaxation.

5. **Embrace Remote Work**: If your job allows, embrace remote work opportunities. Working from home can save commute time and provide a more comfortable work environment, contributing to better work-life balance.

6. **Involve Your Family**: Involve your family in understanding your work commitments and schedules. Open communication can help them support you in maintaining balance.
7. **Combine Work and Personal Goals**: Look for ways to align your work and personal goals. For example, if you enjoy travel, seek sales opportunities that involve travel. Integrating personal interests with work can make your job more fulfilling.

Importance of Self-Care

Self-care is essential for maintaining physical and mental well-being. Prioritizing self-care helps you stay energized and resilient. Here's how to incorporate self-care into your routine:

1. **Exercise Regularly**: Physical activity is a powerful stress reliever. Aim to exercise regularly, whether it's a daily walk, a gym session, or a yoga class. Find an activity you enjoy and make it part of your routine.
2. **Eat Healthily**: Maintain a balanced diet to fuel your body and mind. Avoid excessive caffeine and sugar, and include plenty of fruits, vegetables, and whole grains in your diet.
3. **Get Enough Sleep**: Prioritize sleep to ensure you get adequate rest. Aim for 7-9 hours of sleep each night. Good sleep improves concentration, mood, and overall health.
4. **Practice Relaxation Techniques**: Incorporate relaxation techniques into your daily routine. This can include activities like reading, listening to music, taking a bath, or practicing deep-breathing exercises.
5. **Pursue Hobbies**: Make time for hobbies and activities that you enjoy outside of work. Pursuing

hobbies provides a creative outlet and helps you unwind.

6. **Stay Connected**: Maintain social connections with friends and family. Social support is crucial for emotional well-being. Schedule regular catch-ups with loved ones to stay connected.

7. **Set Aside "Me Time"**: Dedicate time each week for yourself, without work or personal commitments. Use this time to relax, reflect, and recharge.

Conclusion

Maintaining work-life balance is critical for achieving long-term success and well-being in sales. By managing stress and burnout, integrating work and personal life effectively, and prioritizing self-care, you can achieve a healthier and more fulfilling career. Remember, a balanced life not only enhances your professional performance but also contributes to your overall happiness and quality of life. Embrace these strategies to create a sustainable and rewarding sales career.

Chapter 13: Your Journey to Sales Mastery

Embarking on the journey to sales mastery requires dedication, continuous learning, and a commitment to excellence. In this final chapter, we will recap the key concepts covered throughout this guide, provide tips for staying motivated and focused, and suggest resources for further learning to help you continue growing and achieving success in your sales career.

Recap of Key Concepts

Throughout this guide, we have covered essential concepts and strategies to help you excel in sales. Here's a recap of the key concepts:

1. **Understanding the Sales Process**: Recognizing the importance of the sales cycle, setting clear goals, and building a winning attitude are foundational to sales success.
2. **Building a Winning Attitude**: Cultivating a positive mindset, developing resilience, and overcoming rejection are critical components of a successful sales career.
3. **Prospecting Like a Pro**: Identifying your target market, employing effective lead generation strategies, and leveraging social media and technology can significantly enhance your prospecting efforts.
4. **The Art of the Cold Call**: Preparing thoroughly, crafting a compelling pitch, and handling objections confidently are essential skills for successful cold calling.
5. **Mastering the Follow-Up**: Implementing a systematic follow-up process, personalizing your interactions, and providing value in every follow-up can help you build strong relationships with prospects.

6. **Presenting with Confidence**: Crafting compelling presentations, engaging your audience, and using stories and visuals effectively are key to delivering impactful presentations.
7. **Closing the Deal**: Recognizing buying signals, using effective closing techniques, and handling last-minute objections are crucial for sealing the deal.
8. **Time Management for Sales Professionals**: Prioritizing tasks, using time-blocking techniques, and maximizing productivity are essential for managing your time effectively.
9. **Leveraging Technology and Tools**: Utilizing CRM systems, sales automation tools, and data-driven sales strategies can streamline your processes and enhance your sales performance.
10. **Continuous Improvement and Learning**: Staying updated with industry trends, investing in personal development, and learning from every experience are vital for ongoing growth and success.
11. **Maintaining Work-Life Balance**: Managing stress and burnout, integrating work and personal life, and prioritizing self-care are crucial for sustaining a healthy and fulfilling sales career.

Staying Motivated and Focused

Staying motivated and focused is essential for achieving long-term success in sales. Here are some tips to help you maintain your motivation and focus:

1. **Set Clear Goals**: Define clear, achievable goals for your sales career. Break these goals into smaller milestones to make them more manageable and track your progress regularly.
2. **Celebrate Small Wins**: Acknowledge and celebrate your achievements, no matter how small.

Recognizing your successes boosts your confidence and motivation.

3. **Stay Positive**: Maintain a positive mindset, even in the face of challenges. Focus on your strengths, practice gratitude, and surround yourself with supportive and positive influences.
4. **Seek Inspiration**: Find sources of inspiration that resonate with you, such as motivational books, podcasts, or speeches. Learning from others' successes can inspire you to keep pushing forward.
5. **Stay Organized**: Use tools and techniques to stay organized and manage your time effectively. A well-structured schedule helps you stay focused and reduces stress.
6. **Take Breaks**: Regular breaks are essential for maintaining focus and preventing burnout. Schedule short breaks throughout your day and longer breaks to recharge and relax.
7. **Reflect and Adjust**: Regularly reflect on your progress and adjust your strategies as needed. Continuous self-assessment helps you stay on track and improve your performance.
8. **Seek Support**: Don't hesitate to seek support from mentors, colleagues, or professional networks. Sharing experiences and challenges with others can provide valuable insights and encouragement.

Resources for Further Learning

Continuous learning is key to mastering sales. Here are some resources to help you continue growing and developing your sales skills:

1. **Books**:
   o
   "SPIN Selling" by Neil Rackham
   o

"The Challenger Sale" by Matthew Dixon and Brent Adamson

- "Influence: The Psychology of Persuasion" by Robert Cialdini
- "New Sales. Simplified." by Mike Weinberg
- "The Sales Acceleration Formula" by Mark Roberge

1. **Online Courses**:
   - Coursera: Sales courses from top universities and institutions
   - Udemy: Wide range of sales courses covering various aspects of the sales process
   - LinkedIn Learning: Professional development courses focused on sales techniques and strategies

1. **Podcasts**:
   - "The Salesman Podcast" by Will Barron
   - "Make It Happen Mondays" by John Barrows
   - "Sales Gravy" by Jeb Blount
   - "The Advanced Selling Podcast" by Bill Caskey and Bryan Neale

1. **Websites and Blogs**:
   - HubSpot Sales Blog: Insights and tips on sales strategies and techniques
   - Sales Hacker: Community-driven content on sales best practices and innovation

    o

    Close Blog: Practical advice on closing deals and improving sales performance

1. **Professional Associations**:

    o

    Sales Management Association (SMA): Resources and events for sales leaders

    o

    American Association of Inside Sales Professionals (AA-ISP): Networking and development opportunities for inside sales professionals

    o

    National Association of Sales Professionals (NASP): Training and certification programs for sales professionals

Conclusion

Your journey to sales mastery is a continuous process of learning, growth, and adaptation. By staying motivated and focused, leveraging the right resources, and applying the key concepts covered in this guide, you can achieve excellence in your sales career. Remember, success in sales is not just about closing deals but about building lasting relationships, providing value, and continuously improving your skills. Embrace the journey, and you will find fulfillment and success in your sales career.

Chapter 14: Appendix A: Tools and Resources

In the fast-paced world of sales, having the right tools and resources can make a significant difference in your performance and success. This appendix provides a curated list of recommended books, courses, sales software, and apps that can enhance your skills and streamline your sales processes.

Recommended Books and Courses

Books

1. **"SPIN Selling" by Neil Rackham**
   o
   A comprehensive guide on the SPIN (Situation, Problem, Implication, Need-payoff) selling technique, based on extensive research and real-world examples.
1. **"The Challenger Sale" by Matthew Dixon and Brent Adamson**
   o
   Explores the Challenger Sales Model, which focuses on teaching and tailoring sales messages to challenge customers' thinking.
1. **"Influence: The Psychology of Persuasion" by Robert Cialdini**
   o
   A classic book on the principles of persuasion and how they can be applied to sales and marketing.
1. **"New Sales. Simplified." by Mike Weinberg**
   o
   Offers practical advice on prospecting, developing a sales pipeline, and closing deals.
1. **"The Sales Acceleration Formula" by Mark Roberge**
   o

Describes a data-driven approach to building a sales team and increasing sales, based on the author's experience at HubSpot.

1. **"To Sell Is Human" by Daniel H. Pink**
   - Examines the science and art of selling, emphasizing that everyone is in sales to some degree.
1. **"Fanatical Prospecting" by Jeb Blount**
   - Focuses on the importance of prospecting and provides actionable strategies to improve your prospecting efforts.
1. **"Sell with a Story" by Paul Smith**
   -

Teaches the power of storytelling in sales and how to craft compelling sales narratives.

Courses

1. **Coursera: Sales Courses**
   - Offers a variety of courses from top universities and institutions covering different aspects of sales, such as negotiation, sales management, and digital selling.
1. **Udemy: Sales Courses**
   - Provides a wide range of sales courses for all levels, from beginner to advanced, focusing on specific skills like cold calling, closing techniques, and sales automation.
1. **LinkedIn Learning: Sales Courses**
   - Features professional development courses on sales techniques, strategies, and tools, taught by industry experts.

1. **HubSpot Academy: Sales Training**
   - ○

   Free online courses covering inbound sales, sales enablement, and other essential sales skills.
1. **Salesforce Trailhead: Sales Training**
   - ○

   Offers free training modules on using Salesforce for sales, as well as broader sales strategies and best practices.

Useful Sales Software and Apps

Customer Relationship Management (CRM) Systems

1. **Salesforce**
   - ○

   A leading CRM platform that offers extensive customization, automation, and analytics to manage customer relationships and sales processes.
1. **HubSpot CRM**
   - ○

   A free CRM tool that provides robust features for managing contacts, sales pipelines, and customer interactions.
1. **Pipedrive**
   - ○

   A CRM designed to visualize your sales pipeline and help you stay organized and focused on closing deals.
1. **Zoho CRM**
   - ○

   A customizable CRM solution that offers sales automation, analytics, and AI-driven insights.
1. **Microsoft Dynamics 365**
   - ○

Integrates CRM and ERP capabilities to provide comprehensive sales and business management tools.

Sales Automation Tools

1. **Outreach**
   - A sales engagement platform that automates and optimizes sales workflows, including email sequences and follow-up reminders.
1. **SalesLoft**
   - A sales engagement platform that helps streamline and automate communication with prospects through emails, calls, and social media.
1. **Apollo.io**
   - Provides sales automation, prospecting, and engagement tools to streamline your sales processes.
1. **Reply.io**
   - An AI-powered sales engagement tool that automates email outreach and follow-ups, helping you connect with prospects more efficiently.

Lead Generation Tools

1. **LinkedIn Sales Navigator**
   - A powerful tool for finding and connecting with potential leads on LinkedIn, offering advanced search filters and lead recommendations.
1. **ZoomInfo**
   -

Provides access to a vast database of business contacts and company information to help you identify and reach decision-makers.

1. **Hunter.io**
   -

   A tool for finding and verifying email addresses, making it easier to connect with potential leads.

1. **Clearbit**
   -

   Enriches your contact and company data, providing deeper insights into your leads and prospects.

Productivity and Collaboration Apps

1. **Trello**
   -

   A visual project management tool that helps you organize tasks, set priorities, and collaborate with your team.

1. **Asana**
   -

   A project management and collaboration tool that helps you track tasks, manage projects, and improve team communication.

1. **Slack**
   -

   A communication platform that enables real-time messaging, file sharing, and collaboration within teams.

1. **Evernote**
   -

   A note-taking app that helps you capture ideas, organize information, and stay on top of your tasks.

1. **Google Workspace**
   -

A suite of productivity tools, including Gmail, Google Drive, Google Docs, and Google Calendar, to streamline your work processes.

1. **Calendly**
   - A scheduling tool that simplifies the process of booking meetings, allowing prospects to choose available time slots without back-and-forth emails.

1. **Zapier**
   -

An automation tool that connects your apps and automates workflows, helping you save time on repetitive tasks.

Conclusion

The right tools and resources can significantly enhance your effectiveness and efficiency as a sales professional. By leveraging the recommended books, courses, software, and apps, you can stay ahead of the competition, streamline your sales processes, and continuously improve your skills. Remember, the key to success in sales is not just hard work but also working smart and making the most of the resources available to you.

Chapter 15: Appendix B: Templates and Checklists

Having ready-to-use templates and checklists can streamline your sales process, ensuring consistency and efficiency. This appendix provides sales call scripts, follow-up email templates, and a sales pipeline checklist to help you stay organized and effective.

Sales Call Scripts

Initial Cold Call Script

makefile

Copy code

Introduction:

"Hi [Prospect's Name], this is [Your Name] from [Your Company]. How are you today?"

Purpose:

"I'm reaching out because I noticed that [specific reason related to their business or industry]. We specialize in helping companies like yours to [specific benefit]."

Engagement:

"Can you tell me a little about how you're currently handling [related issue]?"

Value Proposition:

"That's interesting. We have helped [similar company] achieve [specific result] by [brief explanation of your product/service]. I believe we could do something similar for you."

Setting the Appointment:

"I'd love to discuss this further and show you how we can help. Are you available for a quick call next week to dive deeper into this?"

Handling Objections:

"I understand that [objection]. Many of our clients initially felt the same way but found that [reassurance and benefit]. Would it be worth 15 minutes to explore if we can add similar value to your business?"

Closing:

"Great, how about [suggest specific date and time]? I'll send you a calendar invite shortly. Thanks for your time, [Prospect's Name]. I look forward to speaking with you."

Follow-Up Call Script

vbnet

Copy code

Introduction:

"Hi [Prospect's Name], this is [Your Name] from [Your Company]. We spoke last week about [specific topic]. How have you been?"

Purpose:

"I'm calling to follow up on our conversation and see if you had a chance to review the information I sent over."

Engagement:

"Do you have any questions or need any clarification about how we can help with [specific issue]?"

Value Proposition Recap:

"To recap, our solution can help you [specific benefit], similar to what we achieved for [similar company]."

Next Steps:

"I'd love to set up a time to give you a more detailed walkthrough. Are you available this week for a quick demo?"

Handling Objections:

"I understand that [objection]. Let me provide some more context. [Provide detailed information and reassurance]. Does that address your concern?"

Closing:

"Fantastic. How about [suggest specific date and time]? I'll send a confirmation email with all the details. Looking forward to it!"

Follow-Up Email Templates

Initial Follow-Up Email

sql

Copy code

Subject: Great Speaking with You, [Prospect's Name]!

Hi [Prospect's Name],

I enjoyed our conversation earlier and appreciated the insights you shared about [specific topic]. I'm excited about the possibility of helping [Prospect's Company] achieve [specific benefit].

Attached is the information we discussed, including [specific document]. If you have any questions or need further details, feel free to reach out.

Would you be available for a follow-up call next week to discuss this further? How about [suggest specific date and time]?

Looking forward to continuing our conversation.

Best regards,

[Your Name]

[Your Position]

[Your Contact Information]

Follow-Up After No Response

vbnet

Copy code

Subject: Following Up on Our Previous Conversation

Hi [Prospect's Name],

I hope this email finds you well. I wanted to follow up on the information I sent last week regarding [specific topic]. Have you had a chance to review it?

I believe that our solution could significantly benefit [Prospect's Company] by [specific benefit]. I'd be happy to answer any questions or provide additional information.

Could we schedule a quick call to discuss this further? How about [suggest specific date and time]?

Thank you for your time, and I look forward to your response.

Best regards,

[Your Name]

[Your Position]

[Your Contact Information]

Post-Meeting Follow-Up Email

vbnet

Copy code

Subject: Thank You for Your Time Today

Hi [Prospect's Name],

Thank you for taking the time to meet with me today. I enjoyed our discussion about [specific topic] and how [Your Company] can help [Prospect's Company] achieve [specific benefit].

Attached is a summary of what we discussed and the next steps. Please review it and let me know if you have any questions or need further clarification.

Looking forward to moving forward with this initiative. If you need anything else in the meantime, don't hesitate to reach out.

Best regards,

[Your Name]

[Your Position]

[Your Contact Information]

Sales Pipeline Checklist

Prospecting

- Identify target market and create a list of potential leads.
- Research each prospect to gather relevant information.
- Prepare customized outreach messages.
- Use CRM to track and manage leads.

Initial Contact

- Send introductory email or make initial cold call.
- Record details of the initial contact in CRM.
- Schedule follow-up calls or meetings with interested prospects.

Qualification

- Ask qualifying questions to determine prospect's needs, budget, and decision-making authority.
- Update CRM with qualification details.
- Categorize prospects based on qualification criteria (e.g., hot, warm, cold).

Presentation

- Schedule and prepare for product/service demonstrations.
-

Customize presentation to address prospect's specific needs and pain points.

-

Use stories, visuals, and data to support your value proposition.

-

Record presentation outcomes in CRM.

Handling Objections

-

Prepare responses to common objections.

-

Actively listen to prospect's concerns.

-

Provide reassurance and evidence to address objections.

-

Update CRM with objection details and responses.

Closing

-

Recognize buying signals and choose appropriate closing technique.

-

Present the final proposal or agreement.

-

Handle any last-minute objections confidently.

-

Confirm the sale and set expectations for next steps.

-

Record the sale and update the sales pipeline in CRM.

Post-Sale Follow-Up

-

Send a thank-you email to the new customer.

-

Schedule a follow-up meeting to ensure customer satisfaction.

-

Provide onboarding materials and support as needed.

-

Ask for feedback and referrals.

Continuous Improvement

-

Regularly review and update sales strategies based on performance data.

-

Attend training sessions and seek feedback from mentors and peers.

-

Stay updated with industry trends and best practices.

-

Set new goals and plan actions to achieve them.

Conclusion

Using these templates and checklists can help streamline your sales process, ensure consistency, and enhance your efficiency. By incorporating these tools into your daily routine, you can focus on building relationships, providing value, and achieving your sales goals. Remember, the key to success in sales is preparation, persistence, and continuous improvement.

www.ingramcontent.com/pod-product-compliance
Lightning Source LLC
Chambersburg PA
CBHW071950210526
45479CB00003B/885